NFL's TOP 10
ROOKIES

by Tom Glave

NFL's TOP TEN

SportsZone

An Imprint of Abdo Publishing
abdopublishing.com

abdopublishing.com

Published by Abdo Publishing, a division of ABDO, PO Box 398166, Minneapolis, Minnesota 55439. Copyright © 2018 by Abdo Consulting Group, Inc. International copyrights reserved in all countries. No part of this book may be reproduced in any form without written permission from the publisher. SportsZone™ is a trademark and logo of Abdo Publishing.

Printed in the United States of America, North Mankato, Minnesota
042017
092017

Cover Photo: Chuck Burton/AP Images
Interior Photos: Ed Kolenovsky/AP Images, 4–5; Al Messerschmidt/AP Images, 7, 21, 27; Steve Mitchell/AP Images, 8–9; Harold P. Matosian/AP Images, 10; Bettmann/Getty Images, 11, 23; Paul Abell/AP Images, 13; Julio Cortez/AP Images, 15; Evan Pinkus/AP Images, 14–15; Tony Tomsic/AP Images, 17; Craig Lassig/AFP/Getty Images, 18, 19; Tony Tomsic/Getty Images Sport/Getty Images, 22; Peter Read Miller/AP Images, 24, 25; AP Images, 26

Editor: Patrick Donnelly
Series Designer: Craig Hinton

Publisher's Cataloging-in-Publication Data

Names: Glave, Tom, author.
Title: NFL's top 10 rookies / by Tom Glave.
Other titles: NFL's top ten rookies
Description: Minneapolis, MN : Abdo Publishing, 2018. | Series: NFL's top 10 |
    Includes bibliographical references and index.
Identifiers: LCCN 2016963096 | ISBN 9781532111433 (lib. bdg.) |
    ISBN 9781680789287 (ebook)
Subjects: LCSH: National Football League--Juvenile literature. | Football--
    --United States--History--Juvenile literature. | Football--United States--
    Miscellanea--Juvenile literature. | Football--United States--Statistics--Juvenile
    literature.
Classification: DDC 796.332--dc23
LC record available at http://lccn.loc.gov/2016963096

Table of
CONTENTS

Introduction

The National Football League (NFL) has lots of great players. Some of them have to wait for their chance to make big plays. But some do it as soon as they get to the NFL.

A rookie can help his team in many ways. He can make big plays or score lots of touchdowns. He might set records and do things no one has seen before.

Most rookies aren't expected to have a huge impact on their new teams. Pro football is much different from the college game. Even a first-round draft pick needs to learn new rules and a new playbook. And he has to adapt to the faster pace and better athletes he'll face in the NFL.

But some players are ready for that challenge from the start. They stand out from the crowd the moment they step onto the field. Read on to learn more about the NFL's top 10 rookies of all time.

10

Edgerrin James was a huge part of the Colts' offense in 1999.

Edgerrin James

The Indianapolis Colts finished the 1998 season with a 3–13 record. Future Hall of Fame running back Marshall Faulk left the team to join the St. Louis Rams. The Colts needed a replacement to join second-year quarterback Peyton Manning and another rising star, wide receiver Marvin Harrison.

The Colts selected Edgerrin James with the fourth overall pick of the 1999 NFL Draft. Some fans were surprised they passed on another star running back, Heisman Trophy winner Ricky Williams.

James quickly proved the Colts right. He rushed for 112 yards and a touchdown in his first game. It was the first of his 10 games that season with at least 100 rushing yards, an NFL rookie record. The Colts won nine of those games.

James became a workhorse for Indianapolis. He led the NFL in rushing attempts, carrying the ball 369 times. Only one other Colts running back carried the ball all year—Keith Elias had just 13 rushing attempts.

James led the NFL with 1,553 rushing yards in the regular season. He finished with 13 touchdowns. He added 62 catches for 586 yards and four touchdowns. James finished second behind

Faulk with 2,139 total yards from scrimmage. That mark was second all-time by a rookie.

James's efforts didn't go unnoticed. He was named the NFL's Offensive Rookie of the Year and was chosen to play in the Pro Bowl. And thanks in part to James's big season, the Colts finished 13–3 and went to the playoffs.

Ben Roethlisberger heads upfield in a downpour during his rookie year. →

Ben Roethlisberger

Ben Roethlisberger started his first season in the NFL as the Pittsburgh Steelers' third-string quarterback. The plan was for him to learn behind two veterans before taking over the job.

That plan changed quickly. Backup quarterback Charlie Batch was hurt during the preseason. Then starter Tommy Maddox was injured during the second game of the 2004 season. Roethlisberger was called to finish the game against the Baltimore Ravens.

It wasn't a great start—his second pass attempt was intercepted, and the Steelers lost.

The rest of the season, however, Roethlisberger and the Steelers were unstoppable. The rookie quarterback led Pittsburgh to 13 straight victories. He was the first quarterback in NFL history to begin his career 13–0 in regular-season starts.

The Steelers had a strong running game and a dominating defense. That took the pressure off Roethlisberger, who finished the regular season with 2,621 passing yards, 17 touchdowns, and 11 interceptions. He broke Dan Marino's NFL rookie records for passer rating and completion percentage. Roethlisberger was named the NFL's Offensive Rookie of the Year.

Roethlisberger's late-game heroics helped keep the winning streak going. He led Pittsburgh to five fourth-quarter comebacks during the regular season. In just his third start, Roethlisberger rallied the visiting Steelers past the Dallas Cowboys with two fourth-quarter touchdown drives. Later in the year at Jacksonville, Roethlisberger completed three passes to set up a game-winning field goal with 23 seconds left.

Roethlisberger added another comeback in his first playoff game. His touchdown pass tied the New York Jets in the fourth quarter before he led the game-winning scoring drive in overtime.

Roethlisberger's rookie year provided a hint of what was to come. The next season he led the Steelers to three road wins in the playoffs. Then they won their fifth Super Bowl, beating the Seattle Seahawks 21–10.

8

Lane delivers the "Night Train Necktie" while playing for the Detroit Lions later in his career.

Dick Lane

Dick Lane didn't like the job he had at a factory. So one day in 1952, he walked into the offices of the Los Angeles Rams and asked for a tryout.

Lane had played football at a junior college in Nebraska before joining the Army. Four years later, all he had was a scrapbook of his high school and junior college experience. It was enough for the Rams to take a chance.

Lane played receiver in junior college, but the Rams switched him to defense. His size, speed, and determination helped make him one of the NFL's best cornerbacks ever.

Lane earned the nickname "Night Train" during his first training camp. Receiver Tom Fears listened to the hit Bobby Morrow song "Night Train" in his room. Lane liked the song and often visited Fears's room to listen

Dick "Night Train" Lane, *right*, intercepts a pass for the Los Angeles Rams in 1952.

NIGHT TRAIN NECKTIE

Lane retired in 1965 with 68 career interceptions, second most in NFL history at the time. But he also was known for his hard tackling. He liked to wrap his arms around opponents' necks and pull them to the ground. The NFL later banned this dangerous tackle, which came to be known as the "Night Train Necktie."

to it. One day a teammate saw Lane listening to the tune and called him "Night Train Lane," and the nickname stuck.

"Night Train" made an immediate impact on the league. He set an NFL record with 14 interceptions during 12 games of his rookie season. The record still stands, despite NFL teams now playing 16 regular-season games.

Lane saved his best for last, too. In the final game of the 1952 regular season, he intercepted three passes and returned one for a touchdown to help the Rams tie for the Western Conference title.

Cam Newton

Cam Newton's skill in passing and running the ball led Auburn University to a national championship in the 2010 college football season. The Carolina Panthers took notice, selecting him first overall in the 2011 NFL Draft. Newton then used those skills to turn the NFL upside-down in his rookie season.

Newton forced fans to take notice from his first professional game. He passed for 422 yards, threw two touchdown passes, and scored another touchdown rushing at the Arizona Cardinals. Even though the Panthers lost, the buzz was spreading.

By the end of the year, a slew of records had fallen. Newton broke Peyton Manning's rookie record with 4,051 passing yards. He also was a force on the ground, running for 706 yards, an NFL record for a rookie quarterback. His 14 rushing touchdowns were the most for any quarterback in NFL history. It all added up to Newton becoming the first player in NFL history to pass for at least 4,000 yards and rush for at least 500 yards in the same season.

The rookie was consistent, too. Newton threw a touchdown pass and ran for a score in the same game eight times during the 2011 season. That tied an NFL single-season record. Not surprisingly he was named the NFL Offensive Rookie of the Year.

A RECORD DEBUT

Newton became the first NFL rookie to throw for at least 400 yards in his first game. Then he posted 432 passing yards a week later in a loss to the Green Bay Packers. He was the first NFL player with back-to-back 400-yard games to begin a career.

6

Odell Beckham Jr.

Wide receiver Odell Beckham Jr. became a national sensation on November 23, 2014. His New York Giants were hosting the Dallas Cowboys in a nationally broadcast Sunday night game. On the first play of the second quarter, Beckham raced more than 40 yards down the field. Quarterback Eli Manning heaved a pass in his direction.

As Beckham got tangled up with Cowboys cornerback Brandon Carr, the ball appeared to be sailing over their heads. That's when Beckham leapt and extended his right arm far above his head, catching the ball with one hand while falling onto his back in the end zone.

The video of Beckham's jaw-dropping, 43-yard touchdown grab went viral. But his rookie season featured much more than just one spectacular catch.

Beckham missed the first four games of the season due to a hamstring injury. But he finished his first season on a hot streak, recording more than 130 receiving yards in his last four games. Beckham set Giants rookie records with 91 catches, 1,305

BECKHAM'S RECORD FINISH

Beckham set a Giants team record for the most catches and receiving yards in one month. He caught 38 passes for 593 yards in November 2014. He broke that record again in December with 43 catches and 606 yards. That was also an NFL rookie record for any month.

Numerous acrobatic catches made Beckham a household name during his rookie season.

yards, and 12 touchdowns. He led the NFL with an average of 108.8 receiving yards per game.

Beckham was the fourth rookie receiver in NFL history to record 1,300 yards. He had nine consecutive games with at least 90 receiving yards to tie an NFL record. And his 91 catches were the second most by a rookie in league history.

Beckham was named the NFL Offensive Rookie of the Year and played in the Pro Bowl. He might be remembered more for his highlight-reel catch, but the former Louisiana State University star put together one of the most remarkable rookie seasons ever.

5

Lawrence Taylor was one of the most feared defensive players in NFL history.

Lawrence Taylor

New York Giants linebacker Lawrence Taylor changed the NFL from the first day he set foot on the field in 1981. Before Taylor came along, a team's best linebacker usually played in the middle. Taylor played outside linebacker. He was big enough to battle offensive linemen and fast enough to cover receivers. He attacked the ball instead of waiting for a play to come to him. He could make plays anywhere on the field.

Taylor also changed the way the NFL kept statistics. Taylor had so many game-changing quarterback sacks that the league started officially tracking sacks in 1982.

Taylor unofficially had 9.5 sacks during his rookie season. He added 133 tackles, broke up eight passes, forced two fumbles, and intercepted a pass.

He immediately made the Giants' defense better. The Giants allowed 425 points and won four games in 1980. With Taylor, they allowed 257 points and went 9–7. The Giants won their last three games to clinch their first playoff berth in 18 years.

Taylor was such a dominant force that teams had to prepare specifically to block him. The eventual Super Bowl champion San Francisco 49ers put their best offensive lineman on Taylor throughout a playoff game. It slowed him down, but he still managed a sack and five tackles.

Taylor won Defensive Rookie of the Year honors. He was also the first rookie to win NFL Defensive Player of the Year Award. He is still the only player to win both awards in the same season.

BIG NICKNAMES

Taylor earned the nickname "Godzilla" at the University of North Carolina because he terrorized quarterbacks like the monster from the famous 1950s films. His Giants teammates were so amazed at the things Taylor did on the field during his first training camp that they started calling him "Superman."

4

Randy Moss

Randy Moss left Marshall University early to enter the 1998 NFL Draft. Experts said he had huge potential as an NFL receiver. But Moss's problems away from the field scared away several teams. Moss slipped to the 21st pick before being selected by the Minnesota Vikings.

He promised to prove that all the teams that didn't draft him were wrong. He started getting his revenge during his sensational rookie season.

Moss used his speed to get away from defenders. That led to a lot of long touchdown catches. At 6-foot-4 he also had the strength and leaping ability to catch the ball in a crowd. Vikings quarterback Randall Cunningham often just threw the ball high and long in Moss's direction, confident his rookie receiver would be the one who would catch it.

The result was Moss catching 69 passes for 1,313 yards and a league-best 17 touchdowns in 1998. That set a record for touchdown catches by a rookie wide receiver.

Moss was an instant hit with Vikings fans.

With Hall of Fame receiver Cris Carter lining up on the same offense, the Vikings racked up a record 556 points and went 15–1 that season.

Some of Moss's best performances that year came on national television. He made five catches for 190 yards against the Green Bay Packers on *Monday Night Football*. That blitz included touchdown catches of 52 and 44 yards.

Moss had another big game in the spotlight on Thanksgiving Day. He caught three passes for 163 yards against the Dallas Cowboys. All three catches went for long touchdowns. He had touchdown catches of 51, 56, and 56 yards in the 46–36 win.

Then, in the playoffs, Moss added 10 catches for 148 yards and two touchdowns during two playoff games. However, the Vikings lost to the Atlanta Falcons in overtime with a trip to the Super Bowl on the line. Still, his amazing season was not forgotten. Moss's incredible catches landed him the NFL Offensive Rookie of the Year Award and a trip to the Pro Bowl.

Jevon Kearse

Jevon Kearse came into the NFL with a great nickname. He was called "The Freak" while playing at the University of Florida because of his athletic ability, speed, and 86-inch (218-cm) wingspan.

Kearse lived up to the nickname during his first year in the NFL, pressuring quarterbacks from his defensive end position. Just one year earlier, the Titans had gone 8–8 and forced a total of nine fumbles. Kearse forced 10 fumbles by himself during his rookie season in 1999. Kearse also set an NFL rookie record with 14.5 sacks that year. Meanwhile, the Titans finished 13–3 and won three playoff games thanks in part to Kearse's play.

Kearse ended the regular season on a tear, recording at least half a sack in 10 straight games. That streak started against the St. Louis Rams on Halloween. Kearse had a sack, a forced fumble, and five tackles against the Rams. His speed and power also had the Rams' offensive linemen a bit jumpy—he drew six false-start penalties that day.

Kearse finished the regular season with a strip sack against the Pittsburgh Steelers. He recovered the loose ball and returned it 14 yards for a Tennessee touchdown.

Kearse was named the Defensive Rookie of the Year after the regular season. He finished second to Tampa Bay's Warren Sapp for the league's Defensive Player of the Year Award. Kearse was also named first team All-Pro and selected to the Pro Bowl.

But his season wasn't done yet. Kearse came up huge in the playoffs as well. He had two sacks in the Titans' playoff opener against the Buffalo Bills. He sacked quarterback Rob Johnson in the end zone for the first two points of the game.

Tennessee advanced to the Super Bowl for the first time in the team's history. The Titans came up short in a 23–16 loss against the Rams, but Kearse ended his rookie year with yet another sack.

2

Gale Sayers slashes his way through the defense for the Chicago Bears.

Gale Sayers

I n 1965 Gale Sayers had a tough decision to make. The Chicago Bears selected him to play in the NFL. But the Kansas City Chiefs also drafted him, hoping to lure the former University of Kansas star to the rival American Football League. Sayers ultimately signed with the Bears, and he went on to score an NFL rookie-record 22 total touchdowns in 14 games.

The man known as the "Kansas Comet" was hard to miss on the field. He was the one juking would-be tacklers with shifty cuts to break into the open field. Then he'd outrun every defender with his knees pumping high as he dashed to the end zone.

Sayers's incredible rookie season included two games in which he scored almost half of his touchdowns. He scored four times, all in the second half, in a 45–37 win against the Minnesota Vikings. Sayers caught two touchdown passes before his 96-yard

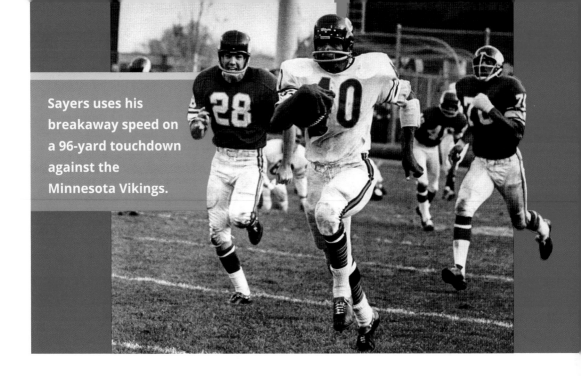

Sayers uses his breakaway speed on a 96-yard touchdown against the Minnesota Vikings.

score on a kickoff return put the Bears ahead for good. He added a 10-yard touchdown run late in the game to seal the Bears' victory.

Two months later, Sayers tied an NFL record when he scored six touchdowns in a game against the San Francisco 49ers. Four of his touchdowns came on the ground, one through the air, and one on an amazing 85-yard punt return in Chicago's 61–20 win. Sayers recorded 336 all-purpose yards in that game, a rookie record that stood until 2007.

Sayers finished the season with 867 rushing yards and scored 14 touchdowns on the ground, trailing only the great Jim Brown in both categories. He also caught 29 passes for 507 yards and six touchdowns. Finally, Sayers tallied 660 yards on 21 kickoff returns and 238 yards on 16 punt returns. He scored a touchdown each way.

He even *threw* a 26-yard touchdown pass in a Bears win against the Los Angeles Rams.

Sayers's 2,272 all-purpose yards were a rookie record at the time, and his 22 touchdowns were an NFL record for 10 years.

1

Eric Dickerson was a graceful and tough running back.

Eric Dickerson

Eric Dickerson's NFL career did not exactly start on a high note. The Los Angeles Rams rookie, who grew up in Texas, was nervous about his debut at a joint practice with the Dallas Cowboys in 1983. He was so nervous that he forgot the plays and had to come off the field.

Dickerson was under a lot of pressure, both to meet high expectations and to disprove his critics. The two-time All-America running back at Southern Methodist University was the second pick in a draft full of future star quarterbacks.

But some NFL scouts didn't think Dickerson would be successful in pro football. At 6 feet, 3 inches and 220 pounds, Dickerson was bigger than most running backs of that era. His critics said his size would slow him down, that he wouldn't be fast enough. His upright running style was unusual, too. Some observers feared it would expose him to big hits from the defense.

None of that stopped Dickerson, who produced the greatest rookie season in NFL history. Dickerson set several rookie and league records on the way

Dickerson's running style cast doubt on his durability, but those fears proved to be unfounded.

to Offensive Rookie of the Year honors, the Pro Bowl, and several other national awards.

Dickerson led the NFL in rushing attempts, rushing yards, and total yards from scrimmage during the 1983 season. His 390 rushing attempts, 1,808 rushing yards, and 18 rushing touchdowns are all NFL rookie records. Dickerson also was a threat in the passing game. He caught 51 passes for 404 yards and two touchdowns. His 20 total touchdowns are the second most by a rookie, while his 441 touches (rushes plus receptions) led the NFL and set a rookie record at the time.

Most of the critics' fears were disproven, although Dickerson's remarkable rookie season wasn't perfect. He fumbled 13 times, just one shy of the most in the league. Then again, when you're touching the ball as often as Dickerson was, you've got more opportunities to lose the ball.

He fumbled six times in his first three games before turning around his season. Dickerson didn't top 91 yards in any of those games, but he broke out in a big way against the New York Jets in Week 4. His 85-yard touchdown run against the Jets was part of a 192-yard day for the rookie. He topped that a week later with 199 rushing yards and three touchdowns against the Detroit Lions.

Dickerson's speed and strength made him a threat to score every time he touched the ball. His style made it all look easy. His upright running and long, graceful strides made it look like Dickerson was gliding down the field.

He helped the Rams make the playoffs in 1983. A year before, the Rams had finished 2–7 in a strike-shortened season. Dickerson's debut helped Los Angeles win nine games and a first-round playoff game at Dallas. After rushing for 99 yards against the Cowboys, Dickerson ended his rookie season on a sour note. In a blowout loss at Washington, Dickerson was held to just 16 rushing yards by the eventual conference champions.

That was just the start of what would eventually be a Hall of Fame career. Dickerson set the NFL single-season record for most rushing yards with 2,105 in 1984. He would go on to have seven straight seasons with at least 1,000 rushing yards.

Dickerson is all smiles as he poses for a photo during his rookie season.

Dickerson turns the corner in the Rams' 1983 playoff victory at Dallas.

It all started with his first season in the NFL. Dickerson, like all these outstanding rookies, made the most of his first opportunity. He made the Rams better. He broke records. And he had an immediate impact on his team and the NFL.

Honorable Mentions

AL "BUBBA" BAKER, DETROIT LIONS, 1978: Quarterback sacks were not yet an official NFL statistic, but Baker unofficially recorded 23 of them during his rookie season. The 6-foot-6, 250-pound Baker blew by offensive linemen and earned Defensive Rookie of the Year honors.

ANQUAN BOLDIN, ARIZONA CARDINALS, 2003: Boldin burst into the NFL with a record debut. He caught 10 passes for a record 217 yards and two touchdowns in his first career game. He finished the season with a rookie-record 101 catches for 1,377 yards and eight scores.

EARL CAMPBELL, HOUSTON OILERS, 1978: The hard-running Campbell tore through defenses all season. He scored three touchdowns against Pittsburgh's famed "Steel Curtain." He added four scores and 199 rushing yards on a memorable Monday night against the Miami Dolphins and led the Oilers to the NFL playoffs for the first time. Campbell finished his rookie season with 1,450 rushing yards and 13 touchdowns.

MIKE DITKA, CHICAGO BEARS, 1961: Ditka was a hard-hitting tight end with speed and soft hands. He had 56 catches for 1,076 yards and 12 touchdowns in 14 games as a rookie. It was the first time an NFL tight end had topped 1,000 receiving yards in a season.

ROBERT GRIFFIN III, WASHINGTON REDSKINS, 2012: Griffin threw for 3,200 yards, 20 touchdowns, and just five interceptions while leading Washington to a division title. He broke Ben Roethlisberger's record for rookie passer rating. He added 815 rushing yards to break Cam Newton's record for rushing yards by a rookie quarterback.

DEVIN HESTER, CHICAGO BEARS, 2006: Hester scored six times on special teams during the regular season. He led the league with 600 punt return yards and three touchdowns, and he added two kickoff returns for touchdowns. Hester also returned a missed field goal 108 yards for a score against the New York Giants. He capped his season by returning the opening kickoff of the Super Bowl 92 yards for a touchdown against the Indianapolis Colts.

RONNIE LOTT, SAN FRANCISCO 49ERS, 1981: Lott had seven interceptions and 89 tackles in his first season. He returned three of the interceptions for touchdowns. He added a 20-yard interception return for a touchdown in the playoffs and helped the 49ers win their first Super Bowl.

ADRIAN PETERSON, MINNESOTA VIKINGS, 2007: Peterson finished second in the league in rushing with 1,341 yards. He also scored 12 touchdowns. He rushed for 224 yards in his fifth game before setting an NFL record in his eighth. Peterson piled up 296 rushing yards against the San Diego Chargers.

BARRY SANDERS, DETROIT LIONS, 1989: Sanders rushed for 1,470 yards and 14 touchdowns a year after winning the Heisman Trophy at Oklahoma State University. He finished 10 yards shy of the NFL rushing title after rushing for at least 100 yards in five of his last six games.

Glossary

all-purpose yards
Yards gained on rushes, receptions, kickoff returns, and punt returns.

draft
A system that allows teams to acquire new players coming into a league.

false start
A penalty that occurs when an offensive player in a set position moves before the ball is snapped.

fumble
When a player with the ball loses possession, allowing the opponent a chance to recover it.

Heisman Trophy
The award given yearly to the best player in college football.

interception
A pass intended for an offensive player that is caught by a defensive player.

line of scrimmage
The place on the field where a play starts.

playoffs
A set of games played after the regular season that decides which team is the champion.

preseason
Games before the regular season that are used as practice and don't count in the standings.

rookie
A first-year player.

For More Information

Books

Bowker, Paul D. *Odell Beckham Jr.: High-Flying Receiver*. Minneapolis, MN: Abdo Publishing, 2017.

Kelley, K. C. *Football Superstars 2015*. New York: Scholastic, Inc., 2015.

Scheff, Matt. *The Best NFL Running Backs of All Time*. Minneapolis, MN: Abdo Publishing, 2013.

Websites

To learn more about the NFL, visit **abdobooklinks.com**. These links are routinely monitored and updated to provide the most current information available.

Place to Visit

Pro Football Hall of Fame
2121 George Halas Drive NW
Canton, Ohio 44708
330-456-8207
www.profootballhof.com

The Hall of Fame is like a museum dedicated to football. There are exhibits on the origins of the game, artifacts from famous moments, and busts honoring the greatest players and coaches ever.

Index

About the Author

Tom Glave grew up watching and playing football. He learned to write about sports at the University of Missouri. He writes about sports for newspapers, websites, and books. He lives in Houston, Texas, and can't wait to play backyard football with his four kids.